Quinn

BY ZAK BELAHMIRA

iLLUSTRATED BY JOHN PATRiCK

Target Skill Consonants Qq/kw/ and Yy/y/

Scott Foresman
is an imprint of

Quinn is a yak.

He is big.

Reg is a little cub.

Quinn and Reg are pals.

Can Quinn hop and skip?
Yes, Quinn can hop and skip.

Can Quinn run?
Yes, Quinn can run.

Can Quinn jump?
No, Quinn can not jump yet.

Can Quinn go in?
No! Stop, Quinn, stop!
You can not go in.

Quinn can not go in.

He will not fit!